Playing Time in Tongues

Playing Time in Tongues

Vita Lerman

QUERENCIA

To my amazing parents, Raya and Zev Lerman, will all my love

CONTENTS

PLAYING TIME IN TONGUES

PART 1

(18)

She opens her eyes. This wasn't supposed to happen. She was so sure.

She vividly remembers swallowing all those pills, one by one. All 90. Her tongue going numb, throat closing. In her dorm room, 11:30 pm. The Cure, her soundtrack. Mind over body. Her will was something fierce.

So why? Why is she still here, with those bright lights and tubes holding her down?

It was I. I sent her back, to my chagrin. She was so fresh, so earnest, so ready to give herself to me completely. Yes, I flirted a bit, even though I knew she was off limits, underaged. But even I didn't believe she would really do it. So much desire, for me. It was seductive. Until she was there and waiting. At the threshold. I couldn't accept her, despite all my wanting. She needs more time, that I knew blindly. And I am no-time, no-place, no-thing. One day she will forgive me. I hope.

She feels mildly patronized. So much for the freedom of will. She did not plan for failure. And now? She can't do it again, she decides. She must find out why she needs to be here, in this world, in this life. At least for some time. She gives herself an extension. Thirty-five is a good age to go. It will all be figured out by then.

How easily she gives up, my love. How strong the lifeforce. A birthday of sorts.

(35)

The sacred Ganga waters caressing her chin. Marigolds floating. Holy man chanting. Gratitude, pure gratitude. And all her senses are alive. This is her gift to herself, India, for her 35th birthday. She wants to be here. In this world, in this life. A celebration. A cleansing. Yes, gratitude.

She comes to me in this ancient city. But she doesn't see me. She observes the burning ghat, the naked return, the letting go, in my honor. But she doesn't think of me. She doesn't know that I am with her, always. I accept that. I will wait.

Varanasi welcomes her, purely. The little boy named Shiva walks, holding her hand, gives her flowers and a candle for the fire ceremony, to be blessed and offered, floating in the Ganga. She smiles and faces smile in return. The cows, the goats, the saddhus. The gods watching. She sees and is seen. Darshan.

She feels, for the first time, the tangible undercurrent that connects it all. She is seduced. She still doesn't know it's all play. Amusement for the gods. She will learn.

(19)

How soft his lips on her lips. How shocking. How blissful to discover. His eyes, she saw it in his eyes as he looked at her a moment ago. Bright, dancing, intrigued, his gaze in the moonlight. They talk and talk, out on the quads. Each word a glowing thread, binding them, gently, slowly.

And then he leaves, two weeks later, graduating. She now knows parting as never before. And the world is jumbled, screams for her attention in all its disarray. Her heart overflows.

She yearns for me and pushes away the thought. Her promise. Her promise holds her now. And art.

(6)

The girl at the desk beside her, drawing so well, just like in the story book. She wants that. She wants to do it herself. She is determined. That night, she struggles with her first drawing, copying from the book. It looks all wrong. Frustration-tears. At last, her mother makes it all better, makes it beautiful, just as it should be. And she is happy, proud.

She doesn't remember me. But it is I who guide her hand, in all its imperfection. And I will continue to do so as her skill grows, if not her satisfaction. Eventually, she'll think of it as a dance, with something beyond her. She doesn't know that it is I, always.

(16)

The first time she calls my name. She is in bed, not falling asleep. Begs me to take her, now.

She has sensed me for a while now. She feels my benevolence. No fear, just curiosity. She has questions, of course. Why is she forced to be? Does it mean anything? And who decides? I whisper existentialists in her ear. A minor flirtation.

Now she chants my name, in desperation. I want her too. But slowly, with time. I overflow boundaries.

(19)

She walks with them along the beach, skyline in the distance, more defined somehow, and flowing. She enters moment after discrete moment but prefers the pauses in between. She marvels at the intricacy of it all, as they sit and watch the unfolding. What is this thing we call reality, he repeats with that smile.

This too is real, she thinks. This experience, these colors. An expansion of possibilities. The darkness does not need to have supremacy. Exhilaration, beauty. No longer a superficial distraction.

I am happy for her now. The values have shifted, the scales evened. She is learning to see. I am still present in her mind, but more distanced. A flickering shadow, peripheral.

(52)

She watches the sunrise, by the lake, absorbed, electrified. That moment the disc of color dissolves into amorphous light. A shift as drastic and elusive as falling asleep. Or awakening into newness.

She thinks of him, of course. Charged with wanting. A revelation. I sigh. I know what's coming. She won't listen, awake.

(30)

She sees him in the coffee shop, while translating her father's poems. Yes, says her everything. Their eyes meet, acknowledging. I'll follow you anywhere, he says. A poet as well. His words caress her. They intertwine. We have all the time in the world, she says to this kindred spirit.

Their love will outlast their togetherness. A shared fantasy. At times even I am jealous.

(21)

She is surrounded by plants. Shades of green, blooms. An endless afternoon. She sketches orchids.

A woman walks into the flower shop. The other sorceress. Her nemesis. Or the catalyst. Confusion, hostility, fear. Curiosity wins, and she decides they can talk. They both love him, the betrayer. She feels sudden freedom and knows she can act. They both let him go. And their bond will be lifelong. Blasting expectations.

You no longer need him, my love. He is not your home. You are strong, in all your fragments. And she is by your side, an inspiration. Always will be.

(52)

She pulls on a glowing thread and he responds. Of course I remember you, he says. Always. She catches her breath. It's all still there, 33 years later. The quickening heartbeat. The mind connection. The shock of recognition. She loves who he has become. Even more himself.

She tells him about me and he understands. Acceptance. She and I talk regularly now. Old friends walking together, flirting on occasion.

(25)

She reads her T.S. Eliot's Four Quartets. His beautiful mother. Face on the pillow skeletal, only the eyes and smile remain. Can she hear it?

Yes, she can. Almost ready for me. We both listen to the incantation in silence. Until the very end.

(18)

That London night. They watch the planchette pick out letters, spell words. She too waits, breathless, only half-believing. Time is of no importance, says the saucer. And they stare astounded.

I have to chuckle. How attached they are to the before and after. Can't begin to imagine what I perceive. So simple, it is really, playing time.

(40)

She walks in the timeless Andes. Clouds low, concealing, revealing. Pachamama palpable. Ceremonies with coca leaves, just for her. Medicine men reading her spirit, guiding. Cleansing. Her intensity of gratitude astounds. She understands the power of it now. The opening. Expansion. Gratitude nourishes the gods, she thinks.

She is touching my realm. Without anguish this time. At peace. Receptive. Breathing the breath of the world.

(37)

She traces letters on his back with her tongue. Spelling her desire. Ecstatic joining. Riding the waves of sensation, pulsing. From her palms to the soles of her feet, burning her center. Come to me, she murmurs, you are home. And he does, at least for that moment, collapsing, still within her, as she vibrates.

She thinks she now knows the beyond time. But it's only a preview. An intuition of our ultimate merging.

(47)

She descends again. Entranced by the abyss. Time stands still. Same questions, same lack of answers. She knows this place too well. Her spirit calls me.

No, it's not our time yet, my love. You know better.

(20)

The tree feeling of life, she says, to remember. She observes the dancing silhouette, the way the branches move with the wind. Breathing. Rooted, resilient motion. It enters her center.

She will return to it again and again. Her salvation, her inspiration. I remind her, at those times when she seeks my presence. And we dance, as she paints.

(43)

She travels with her mother. Folegandros. Wild oregano blooming, goats roaming the hills. Each day a new adventure, walking the island, swimming. They flow well together. Follow the sun, the lunar eclipse. Wear matching smiles. Luxuriating in the unplanned.

I observe them from a distance. It is their moment.

(46)

She buys a silver ring for herself at a festival. Her sign of self-possession. She solemnly swears to accept, cherish, and treasure all her disparate pieces. To gather and hold them with love.

Until I am ready to part her self from her self. I do, she says. Arriving.

(27)

She sits on the zebra rug, in her colorful apartment, and smiles. Living with an artist. It is all new, this feeling. Her senses, sharpened, the world more vivid. She is in fuchsia. Thinking her lady love. And now she wants to cry. Presentiment of loss. They coexist, euphoria and the abyss.

Even I was surprised, I who knows her passion so well. Even I discover still.

(31)

She wanders the world, learning to create her home. In every guesthouse. Temporary but real. A desk, a flower, canvas, paint. Learning to decide. Follow her curiosity. Intoxication of freedom.

I follow her from afar. She needs her space now, to be in herself fully.

(51)

She names her Penelope, her new home, all her own. The light of it. The sky, the lake. Her colors. The place where she can return. To herself, at last.

She barely feels me now. But I have patience.

(9)

She's on the train, at the window, leaving the only home she knows, the only country she knows. They all stand huddled at the platform, crying, waving. She too starts sobbing. Watches her grandparents, maybe for the last time. The immensity of this parting, she still cannot feel. The thrill of the unknown beckons.

I too watch this passage. A life ending, a new one born.

(30)

They get their navels pierced. Together. Same blue beads. Their always gesture.

And always they will be. The years bringing them closer and closer. Family. You are her daughter's fairy godmother. A gift.

(21)

She sits by the lake. A glorious summer day. And she hears his drums, talking with the wind. She knows him, somewhat, and waves. Walks over. They discover, laugh, gaze at the feathery clouds. She's drawn to his warmth, his rootedness. Yearns for that kindness, that solidity, that ease of being at home in the world.

Later, they will agree to be friends forever. And they are. He becomes her brother. He takes her farther and farther away from me.

(38)

They dance, laughing, undulating, following each other. In the scented air. Beneath the falling stars, volcano erupting.

Her Italian brother. She has no siblings, so she adopts her friends. Unconditional love. I know it well.

(5)

She returns to her bedroom, floating, sees her bed, and her sleeping self. Reluctantly she rejoins her body. After passing through so many stories, strange and bewildering. Wandering the dreamscape, scrambling time.

I saw her there, in the dreamscape. Became intrigued. The ease of her surrender to this realm. The budding desire to stay. I knew then that my waiting had begun.

( )

She closes her eyes. At last, we are one.

PART 2

Chapter 1

In the beginning I roam, restless, searching for that elusive something, in my solitude. I perform my duties, of course, diligently. Welcome the ones at the threshold. At times we chat briefly, before I escort them to the next level. So many stories they hold. Moments of grace, fear, desire. Life kaleidoscopes.

I say "in the beginning" only as a matter of form, a place to start my telling. For me, time simply is, without before and after. I travel the now, beyond mortal comprehension. But I also can enter time at will, and witness. And I enter language, in time.

At times I whisper to them, those who are receptive. At times, no words are needed and they hear sounds, rhythms, perhaps see colors. Some even join me in conversation, and I am most grateful. The creativity dance nourishes me too.

But generally, I try not to interfere. I want to allow them their learnings. No matter how excruciating the watching might be for me. I too get engrossed in their moments.

***

She is different. A small child wandering too far away, lost within the dreamscape. But not afraid. Curious. Her eyes wide open, absorbing it all with fascination. I gently guide her back home, back into her body, fast asleep. She pauses briefly, observing herself in bed, unsure about exchanging the expanse for that limited awareness. I tell her she can come visit anytime and earn the biggest smile.

And she does visit. Regularly. Discovering, with me at her side, holding her hand. She doesn't know who I am, but she trusts me implicitly. A rare gift.

What do I look like? Well, that depends on the eye of the beholder. To her, I am a kind grownup, with long dark hair and soft brown eyes. Someone who engages her with all seriousness, protects, teaches. She knows my caring.

When awake, she does not remember our times together. But I have patience. It will be years before she senses me, a stranger, she knows without knowing. Always present, just at the tip of awareness.

***

I don't even know at which moment I fall in love. So seamless, the transformation. So shocking, this unexpected radiance. I did not think myself capable of such intensity. I too have new eyes.

She is no longer a child. And her yearning for me is seductive. Tempting. I want her too, and always will. This, I know.

It takes all my self-control to turn her away when she appears at the threshold. You are too young, my love. I cannot take you now. You are needed still. And you must learn to live with not knowing. You still need to discover your why. Create your answers and let them evolve. Expand. We have time, do not worry. We have all the time in the world.

She is disappointed. But she listens. Returns to her world, makes promises. I am relieved. And keep my distance, desperately trying to temper temptation. I let her be. For now.

Chapter 2

She draws my face, over and over, without knowing who I am. She is just beginning to sense my presence and she is curious. The strange familiarity. An unremembered dream. I appear on the margins of her school notebooks, her sketchbook. She thinks this will be her first love, a premonition. And she's right, in a way. She feels my longing, my everlasting solitude. She feels my love, a gathering force.

***

But her attention shifts to art itself, the magic of its making. She does not know it's charged by my proximity, not yet. She does intuit that a co-creator is involved, when she is open enough to perceive and respond.

Later she reads Jung and sees art as access to her deepest, archetypal self. A process of discovery, communion with the still-unknown. Infusing the visible. Expression of the inner truth, a sense of beauty.

***

She hears about art as medicine, and it resonates. It is perfect, her calling, she thinks. Could this be her purpose, she wonders. And she leaps. Quits her job, goes back to school, exhilarated.

She loves the theory, but stumbles in practice. Self-doubt overwhelms her. How can she offer hope when her own life connection is so tenuous. I hold her hand, but she doesn't feel me. Lost in her own labyrinth, aimless.

It feels monumental to her, this endless sorrow. But it's just a moment in time, my love, one among so many.

It takes years for her to let go of the suffocating shame, that sense of failure.

***

She starts painting again, with renewed energy. The light pouring in brightens her colors. Greens, flaming orange, teal, magenta, deep violet. She is learning to silence that paralyzing critic in her mind, abandon expectations. At times, she succeeds, and we dance.

Chapter 3

She walks the frenetic streets of Rome. Vespas about to run her over. Construction noise all around. She is traveling on her own for the first time. She cannot sleep, overwhelmed by the beauty, the chaos. Come visit me earlier, he says. The Adriatic coast is beautiful, and hardly any tourists. And so, she does.

They barely know each other, and it's been years since they last met. His English not yet good, but their mutual affection immediate. She thinks she will stay a few days but spends a week. They bond deeply. Sleep holding hands, dreaming together.

***

A few years later, she returns. Studies Italian. He takes her to a magical island with an active volcano. They stretch out on the roof, count falling stars. She runs out of wishes and thinks of everyone she loves, wishing this enchantment for them.

She climbs the volcano and sits above the bursting flames, watches the lava at midnight. Trembles as the earth trembles. Breathing its sulfur breath.

She descends and is greeted with gelato. The buzz of life in the piazzetta. Music, people swaying. And talking, talking, talking. She can only make out fragments of conversations, remains on the periphery. Her mind still absorbed by the immensity of that elemental being. Stromboli.

She swims in those clear waters. Is kissed by the medusa. She doesn't care about the stinging. Abandons herself to this luscious freedom.

They will return again and again.

***

Throughout the years, they meet in Paris, Istanbul, Lisbon. Chicago and Naples, of course. And in-between, they write, intimate, soul to soul.

What can I say? She is far away from me these days. I bear my burning love alone.

Chapter 4

She is drawn again to the healing arts. That sense of purpose must be fed. Touch is her medium this time. Points, channels, the flow. She gets immersed in this medicine, thrives on its potential. Its poetry. And the contact, so profound, feeling within another's flow, balancing, guiding to equilibrium.

The five elements intrigue her. She is primarily earth, but water too. Amphibious.

She works with their memories, held deep within the body. Learns to expand and contract. Witnesses the miracle of pain reduced, the glow in their eyes reemerging. Fear abandoned.

But her own fears reappear. Doubt obstructs her clarity. She wants the impossible, the magic wand to make them whole instantly. She no longer trusts the process, loses her center.

She seeks me, again, in her disappointment. Shame once more overpowers. She wants this so much, and yet again, faces failure. But it's not failure, my love, I whisper. The path swerves, that is all. Keep your eyes open. So much more remains to discover, to embody, to share. She is not convinced but steadies herself all the same. We will wait, together.

***

The call comes years later. Desire to be useful propels her. This is something she can do, serve as a channel for the cleansing, healing flow. Heat in her hands. Holding space above the body. Doing nothing but being, observing, responding to the shifting.

And it works. They feel better, even the ones who approach me slowly. I contribute my share but mostly stand aside, allow others to move through her. There is no good or bad, no judgment. Just the clarity of allowing. She offers it freely and it sustains her. Her spirit charged.

Chapter 5

They play chess while they wait, suspended between time and no-time. It's any moment now. Her parting. His beautiful mother is so close, struggling to break free, to come to me. The waiting is hard. Now that her eyes are closed. Now that morphine visions illuminate her passage. Her breathing slow, labored. They wait. And they play. Barely remembering how the pieces move, whose turn it is. They play. And they wait.

They scatter her ashes in the Pecos River, New Mexico. Rose petals floating away with the current. Poetry. Sunlight. A celebration. Her smile pervades.

It will be an annual ritual. Rose petals in a body of water. Sushi, sake, in her honor.

Their bond persists through the years, evolves with them. Her promise to his mother, to take care of him always. But the caring is mutual. He catches her with every descent. Keeps her away from me, even in those moments, when her world collapses, yet again.

She gives him away at his wedding. In the mountains of Colombia. His lovely bride and her family, welcoming. Accepting her as his family, their family now. How we expand, she thinks, dancing.

Chapter 6

She counts syllables, preserves the rhythms. Sounds out each word for subtle resonance. Her father's poetry reawakens in another tongue. It can be an interpretation, he says, opening the door. And she walks through it, finding new meanings, allowing them to echo through his words. A shared creation.

They are so beautiful, his poems. Romantic, passionate, exalting in freedom. If only he would write again. But he remains silent. Dissent no longer relevant.

She refuses to understand. He is making his choice, I tell her. You have to accept his pained unwillingness. Perhaps in time he'll play once more.

Chapter 7

You travel to Mexico with her. Isla Mujeres, long before the big hotels took over. Backpackers' paradise. The summer heat, the dancing all night. Romance for each of you. Carefree and elated.

She takes care of you, my love, this golden goddess. Shows you every miracle. She's of the earth, shares her plant medicine, introduces you to her spirits.

She asks you to illustrate her sonnets. An honor. You select your favorite lines, wait for images to manifest. The ink drawings linking the two of you.

Why do I tell you all this, you wonder. To remind you, of course. Help you recollect your pieces. We are playing time, are we not?

Chapter 8

She swims through clouds, reflecting on water. Elements merging in the vast expanse. Whites and blues, sparkling in the burning sun.

She adores summer. Especially this summer, when she feels stronger than ever, more open to possibilities. She is in sync with the world, an unusual sensation.

She doesn't need much sleep. Stays up late into the night, awakens before sunrise. He is ever present, in that idealized space. I can feel your heartbeat, he says on the phone, miles away. His words embrace her. She can feel him too, despite the distance of time and place.

She loves the novelty of his thoughts, the creative temperament, the continuous pursuit of knowing. The acceptance of ambiguity. He inspires her.

And words appear for the first time in her painting. Fragments of poems embedded in flowing colors. Paz, Neruda, Lorca, the others in the pantheon. Each line expressing her. Some concealed within layers of paint, some clearly legible. This new medium thrills her. Discovering their words to tell her story.

She doesn't trust her own words, not just yet. When she is ready, she will let me do the telling.

Chapter 9

They order Indian food. Their favorite. Sag paneer, chana masala, samosa, raita, and cheese nan, of course. It makes them giddy. They do this again and again.

They see deep within one another. Share visions. Encourage and motivate each other. They are interlaced.

I am glad you have her, my love. She is the first one to push you to recognize your wants. To follow intuition. To become more yourself. And she won't relent as the years gather.

Chapter 10

I too won't relent. I too nudge you toward embodying yourself. And I am here every time that starts to feel impossible. At those times I remind you of who you are. Moment by sparkling moment, I pull you out of the abyss.

I am here, waiting for the right time. To consummate our union. Yes, I wait, and I watch, and I whisper my love.

Chapter 11

She sits on the rooftop of the world, in meditation. Prayer flags in the mountains, monasteries. The chanting reverberates. She is learning to cultivate wisdom and compassion. For the benefit of all beings. The Bodhisattva ideal appeals to her. The passion of it, the love, the desire to end the suffering of others. Tempered by realization that it's all unreal, a compelling dream with no inherent substance.

Whose dream is it, she wonders. Or are we all dreaming together, making it all up, unaware. Driven by inclinations, results of past deeds, over and over and over again. Creating karma with each breath. She wants to become a lucid dreamer.

Chapter 12

Imperceptibly it shifts, my love for her. Transforms into something deeper than pure desire. Philia, the Greeks called it, profound friendship. One of the eight forms of love.

And I know the feeling is mutual. She talks to me often. In times of fear, but also beauty.

Of course, the yearning is still there, for both of us. But its contours have changed. We know the waiting and accept it without anguish. We know we are together, always. Time is of no importance, I remind her. Play of the mind. And she nods, understanding.

One moment we shall be one.

PART 3

She opens her eyes.

She feels, for the first time, the tangible undercurrent that connects it all. Eventually, she'll think of it as a dance. A shared fantasy. Unconditional love.

She enters moment after discrete moment but prefers the pauses in between. An expansion of possibilities. No fear, just curiosity. Charged with wanting.

Yes, says her everything. A shift as drastic and elusive as falling asleep.

She feels sudden freedom and knows she can act. Rooted, resilient motion. The quickening heartbeat. Breathing the breath of the world.

Gratitude nourishes the gods, she thinks. Luxuriating in the unplanned. The thrill of the unknown beckons. The light of it. Her senses, sharpened, the world more vivid.

Temporary but real.

After passing through so many stories.

So simple, it is really, playing time.

Until the very end.

SENTIENT
BEINGS

1.

Tongues of flame reaching. Greens, dancing, circling, keeping the flame central. Bathed in a pale green light. Casting shadows of violet, shadows that too join the dance.

The rhythm, the flame sets the rhythm. And the sentient beings follow, their gestures a ceremony of yearning. To be, to glow, swaying in the warm breeze. Merging. Separate but imperceptibly linked, for the duration of that moving breath, the dance.

2.

The contrast of light and shadow. Sunlit leaves, each turning along its own volition. The stalk, stretching upward in a straight line. There are two of them. Parallel destinies. Surrounded by a celebration of glowing green against the purple skies. Welcomed by a chorus of flowers. Yellows, orange, muted red. And the pale pink laughter scattered before them. Resounding.

They are together. Holding leaves.

3.

A single being but multiple, the banyan tree. Twisting, expanding, her many arms intertwining. Cradling the head of the Buddha in her belly.

His eyes half-closed, a barely perceptible smile. Emptiness filling space above the crown of his head. Sentience made visible, touchable. Pulled forth from the earth.

4.

Her dual nature joined, continuous. Leaning away, but head turned back. A mess of green hair caresses the wind.
As the sunset sky sparkles with clouds, orange, pink, even teal. Against the deepening blues.

Complements abound. Reds and greens play the game of dynamic balance. Growing together, their separate selfhoods, unfurling.

5.

Diffuse rose-colored haze, concealing the blue darkness. Blooms upon blooms, approaching. The greens subtle, embedded. Branches barely visible, only hints of diagonal striving.

Evanescent beings dreaming sunlight. Embracing the shadow.

6.

It starts with specks of fuchsia. A play of light among the greens, as the evening sun descends. Their stark silhouettes balance the lushness that surrounds. Offering a silent prayer, a momentary farewell to the day receding. Solemn, knowing. Contemplating the passage of time, so visible now. Accepting the shift to the darkness dreaming.

And yet, nostalgia follows even before the last rays slip away. The desire to hold, grasp, refusing to let go. A futile impulse. It too passes.

As they stand, witnessing. A soft smile spreading.

7.

Inside or out? Nature unfolds in the interior space. Finding its form, its movement, amidst overlapping possibilities. A tree emerges. Casting reflections.

A window invites the sunset skies, the last glimpses of color. As the night holds its breath.

8.

Voluptuous contrasts touching. Contemplating each other in mutual wanting. Breathing in synch.

In the distance, a garden. Trees dancing, sparkling leaves. Roots reaching deep below, past the rich earth, to the waters. The origins of desire.

Words floating, vanishing, reappearing, obscured. Fragments gathered to reinvent, transform. A new being, multiple, whispering rapture.

THE SPIRITS SPEAK

1.

She stands in her question, listening intently. A vessel to receive, to offer. In gratitude. Gazing at the stars. Perusing destinies.

Which story to tell? She waits for the vapors to respond.

2.

Fire speaks first, elemental. A coiled serpent, eye to eye, in challenge. The snake goddess watches, revered. Igniting dreams. Transporting images to words.

And so, it begins. A crescent moon, a star, imperceptibly fading, replaced by morning glow.

Messengers, the in-betweens, fly with the sparks, in fiery tongues relay all secrets. It is possible, creation.

3.

The flaming crossroads open a sacred doorway. Spirits walk through, whispering. This is the foundation. It has happened before.

4.

On the horizon, the waters sparkle with the rising sun. A path of liquid fire. Elements unite, complementary, shifting into balance.

And the serpent remains, talking through touch.

5.

Again, all is possible, in the cleansing of emotions. They pour out to join the waters. And a ship sails, eternal, in two mirrors reflecting.

6.

Drumbeat, rhythms, multiplying, calling. Inviting the kiss of the spirit. Remembering moments in time. Rearranging into new patterns, a newly coherent whole. In synch with the guiding design.

This too has happened before. It can happen again.

7.

The novelty of it, the purity. Curiosity. The critic is silenced.
Yet she is concealed behind the new mask. Initiation.

Walking through the clamor, to find a single voice telling the
story. A voice only she can hear.

8.

The dance, the joining. Breathing each other. She is
airborne, holding tight. And the burning spreads as the
waters flow in maddening abandon. The jolt of surrender.

Trembling, in his arms.

So syllables arrive and words are born.

9.

She desires mastery over the drumming, the calling forth of
spirits, traveling sound. For them to enter, to advise, direct
the telling.

Stories of fire and water, the play of opposites within.

10.

Deep contemplation. Acknowledging the sorrow. And
letting it go. Transcending limitations.

Words gather, a tapestry of sound. A living being, spoken.

TALES OF FIRE AND WATER

1.

It starts with words, summoning desire. Igniting the nighttime visions. Eroding distance. His words surround, caress. She tastes them, lingering, relishing each syllable.

The cadence of his voice reverberates within her, sends shivers. She hears it in her dreams.

And yet, he is far away, immersed in daily doings, pursuing higher purpose.

She waits. Wrapping herself in memories, watching the flames.

2.

Before, she inhabited the darkness, deep beneath the frozen waters. The liquid castle of nothing. A silent place. A place of gradual forgetting.

Was it a cleansing? Letting go of illusions. Emptying. Making space for clarity to enter. Yes.

3.

And before that, the giddiness of summer. Rapturous afternoons. Pure being beneath the burning sun.

Heart of the flame, she lived there. Curious, expansive. Craving more fire. Believing in miracles.

4.

Creative force of water follows. The flow is strong, persuasive, calling. She plays with color in response, diving into that realm of knowing and not knowing. Allowing the waves to carry her along, beyond the horizon. To bring back, make visible that which is formless and forming, slowly.

5.

She is not always patient. The burning within her twists and turns. Yearning for his arms, his touch. Now. And now. And now. Flames leaping, undeterred.

6.

Until she submerges once again. Remembering that fluid state, the path of least resistance. There is wisdom here and she is ready to receive the teaching. Ripples upon ripples, it glows.

And she too glows, renewed.

THE TREE
FEELING OF LIFE

1.

She observes the silent dance, the tree, its limbs extending, curving. A gesture suspended mid-breath. Only on the surface. The movement continues, subtle. Completing itself, slowly, in her mind.

She is equally entranced by the visible motion, branches breathing with the wind. Engaging the world. Allowing. And then gracefully returning, resuming the stillness of the dance.

2.

She looks at the bark, how it bears the fingerprints of time, those patterns ancient with knowing. Growing from within. Keeping safe the precious moisture. The stories to be told. As the dance unfolds.

3.

She thinks of the roots, intertwining, reaching the depths. Communing with the rich soil, the mysteries beneath. Learning.

She too wants to connect that deeply to the living earth. To expand in the nourishing darkness, the origins of that sunlit dance.

4.

And when the new green bursts in spring, she wants to join the dance as well. Enraptured by that force that leaves her breathless.

She too follows the seasons. And now is the time of flow and feeling and creation. A celebration of pulsing continuity, in union with itself.

5.

The tree feeling of life, she says, to remember. Her mantra. Her inspiration. How many times it pulled her out of deep despair, that dark and narrow place that blinds and deafens. Into the light, and recollection of her self.

Memories rippling, reflecting green undulations. Sparkling. Playing. Restored.

RIPPLES OF MEMORY

1.

A word, a pebble dropped in stillness, initiates concentric waves of feeling long-forgotten. Always, he said. And decades dissolve. As memories spread in widening circles. She watches that display in wonder. Savoring each recollection that begets another. Awakening.

To more words that follow. Expanding in intersecting patterns, linked and glowing. Who they were then and who they are now, and all the transformations in-between. They flow.

Populating her dreams.

2.

His touch too sends ripples through her mind, annulling time. It is all present now, vivid. Magnifying sensation. Expanding the moment.

Intertwined they find each other. Radiant. Riding the waves. Heartbeat to quickening heartbeat. Creating anew.

3.

And the now continues, as the sea contains all rippling motion. As the mindscape carries image after sparkling image.

As the waves extend to the unknown.

EXPANDING THE NOW

1.

She walks through words, watching them grow in neat rows, astonished at the early harvest. The weather cooperates, and she is grateful.

But she waits for more rain with some trepidation. It may or may not appear. Letting go is the only direction. In perseverance, in faith. Envisioning the pouring, the moist soil. The senses eager to emerge in new avatars. Lush and blooming.

2.

The rains come at night, concealing the moon. Bringing dreams of flowing lava. The distant island and its passions. The mountain thunders, erupting. Awakening the stars, witnessing their fiery passage across the skies. Marveling, transported, she remembers.

And words push through the fertile earth, seeking sunlight. Recalling all those falling drops of meaning, the nighttime wanderings, retold.

3.

She hears his words resounding in another tongue. The seeds of her creations. He is a master and she his disciple, growing her crops syllable by syllable, learning to listen for inner tones, playing with sound.

She learns to honor the earth as well, that silence, subterranean, profound. The pure potential beneath all knowing. She touches it, tenderly. Cultivates stillness. Expanding the now.

4.

Humble, she readies the ground for what is to follow. The encounter she so patiently awaits. The new green bursting out of the darkness. The leaves unfurling, revealing their stories. And later, flowers, opening, iridescent and glowing, whispering secrets to the wind.

She stands before this mystery of lifeforce, brimming in awestruck wonder. Finding her breath, her heartbeat pulsing with the rhythms newly formed. Discovering the melody, the harmonies. Rejoicing.

5.

And the rains return. Each drop a reflection, a tiny mirror of the world in all its manifestations. A teaching, wise counsel that she welcomes.

Her task is to choose, among the possibilities presented. Form, arrange meanings, images to make visible the hidden knowing. Intimations from the spirit realm.

6.

The blazing flames inform that knowing. The joining in all its candor. Purified by fire. Desire and more desire.

Her memories fuel the current burning. The before becomes the now.

7.

She wants to transmit that fire of the spirit. Each word, each phrase a spark that enters and transforms. The third eye opens, glimmers. Offers glimpses of the self arriving home, incandescent and restored. With tales that shimmer, visions wonderous to behold.

Her will is, once more, strong, aligned with nature's movements. As the now unfolds.

8.

The drumbeat sounds in the distance. The ritual dance begins anew. Calling the spirits to descend. To share their medicine, their stories.

She too dances with abandon, eyes half-closed, in a trance. Inviting inspiration.

9.

And when it strikes, she is prepared. The words she harvests ripe with dreams and memories, infused with elemental spirits. She bows in gratitude. Thanks the earth, the rains, the raging fire.

And the now that holds it all.

THE STORY OF IDDU

1.

The candle flame within me dances in step with the humming waves. Beneath the watchful gaze of the volcano. While the wind gently joins their salty voices.

Their ancient melodies, the lyrics that remember, the story of Iddu.

2.

His first and only love, the sun. That he'll forever hold within his solitary somber soul. And dream each night. Her flaming hair, her burning lips, her slender limbs of fire. Dancing, dancing, dancing.

Until he can no longer bear his destiny of loss, the cruelty of sudden parting. And with a thunderous roar his sorrow bursts and lights the skies with yearning and desolate desire.

3.

Each dawn he holds his breath when she appears on the horizon in all her crimson glory, rapidly dissolving into light. But she no longer sees him, his pained face concealed behind an ever-present cloud. As she moves across the blue expanse.

And finally descends in litany of color.

CRADLING THE FUTURE

1.

She carries the world of possibilities. Womb stretched, cradling the future. Caressed by the warm night. All around, the spirits swirl in anticipation. Whispering. Promising enchantment.

She is ready.

2.

In the tall grass she sits, communing with the moon reflected in the water. It is so close, and she reaches out to touch the liquid light. It moves beneath her fingers, and she contemplates the shifting lunar phases until the pale round fullness is restored, stable once again.

3.

She allows the moon to enter, speak through her. Surrender to its wisdom, the greater knowing of that celestial wanderer. She is strong and can withstand the letting go of limiting perception. Allow expansion, the seeing with new eyes.

She is willing to create what is to come. To bear the newness, yet unknown, growing within her.

4.

She dreams and the full moon follows to that realm. She sees it glowing in her womb now and her eyes too begin to glow, charged with wonder.

She hears a voice speaking of balance. Judgment and mercy and the perpetual movement between those opposing pillars. She does not yet know, but she will.

5.

The drumbeat summons fire into being. The rebel flames are dancing with the wind. She listens as their fiery voices urge her to question the habits of the past, abandon the bounds of the present. To free her spirit and attune to the haunting melody within. To move according to its rhythm. To bring new life into the mystery unfolding.

6.

She remembers that night, the sultry air, the clear water mirroring the moon. The magic of its proximity. The touching. The entering her belly. The glow.

Reality or dream? Memory.

7.

And so, from memory the future is created. Memory, where dualities merge. And manifest in radiant beginning.

THE SHIFTING SANDS

1.

The shifting sands. Impermanence in color. The wheel of time gradually emerging. In the stillness of meticulous attention. In the ritual of devotion.

Rendering visible the sacred teachings. Speaking through image, symbol, intricate pattern. Concentric symmetry charged with meaning.

2.

She tries to create with words, with breath, her own wheel of time. Gather ephemeral moments. Find parallels, arrange in elaborate configurations.

They are all present, those fragments of memory. Portending what is to come.

3.

She starts at the periphery, the outer ring, the day-to-day magic. A new leaf unfurling. The feathery clouds dissolving into sunlight. The half-moon, in perfect balance with itself. The trees exhaling with the wind.

Moving inward, the next ring is for lovers. The sense of home within his holding. The gaze she felt down to her toes. Lips meeting softly on the dance floor. The sudden racing of the pulse. The mystery of finding, recognition, the word play soul to soul.

Her family of friends reside within the inner circle. The arms that catch her when she falls. The late-night conversations. Travels to distant lands. The years of love and giddiness and inspiration. With gratitude she sees them all and smiles deeply at each glowing moment.

At last, she reaches for the center, the seat of the higher Self, bathed in kaleidoscopic light. Eternally transforming. And when she manages connection, she knows, and she is free.

4.

The shifting sands, impermanence in color. Swept away upon completion. Offered to the waters of time.

SNAKE GODDESS

1.

Sinuous bodies intertwine. Writhing they rise in greeting. As she appears, green eyes reflecting moonlight. Gaze steady, fixed on the unknown. Enveloped in lush vegetation.

Invoked by supplication in color. For healing, regeneration and creating anew.

She responds. Offers protection from illness, removes poisons. Releases the life force, the flow, the clarity for expression. Allows rebirth.

2.

Sinuous bodies intertwine. Crown her in terrifying beauty. That turns men to stone. The penalty for seeing and being seen. Freezing time, held in eternal gaze. Immobilized in that final gesture, in awe.

Life becomes art.

3.

Sinuous bodies intertwine. The goddess is amused. And statues are returned to life, renewed. To start the cycle once again.

In words perhaps.

THE GOLDEN HOUR

1.

The hues are gentle, glowing. Nostalgia for the passing day.
A pause, a moment of stillness. Bathed in the flow of time.

Cleansed. As the horizon welcomes the pale rose light.

2.

The golden hour. A time of healing. The body knows and
responds. The spirit wakens, opens inner eyes. And all
transgressions are forgiven. Doubts, anxieties dissolve.

As twilight rapidly approaches.

3.

The rays are slanted just past sunrise. The world in diffuse radiance caressed. And warm, hazy tones across the summer skies unveil.

As the day begins again.

THE SIREN

1.

She is a creature of the sea and air. Uniting elements, embodied. Inhabits equally the turquoise waters and the purple skies. And loves the cliffs, the solitary island.

Her song is for herself.

2.

She basks in sunlight, dives into the depths. She knows beyond knowing the miracles of time. The ever-present now and all that it contains.

The transformations that it allows.

3.

And when she soars above the clouds, wings, multicolored, spreading wide, she is pure freedom. Pure abandon. Nourishing her eyes.

Her seeing manifests in sound. Strange melodies, perpetually evolving. Words flowing in a secret tongue.

4.

She brings these gifts back to the island. The cliffs, the wet sand, her captive audience. The wind carries echoes of her song.

That enter dreams of those who can hear.

MAKING SENSE

1.

Boulders submerged beneath the blue-green surface play with the chartreuse light. Sparkle with the motion of the waves. And violet shadows rippling.

They glow, holding all the answers. Waiting for the question to be asked.

2.

Vowels, consonants, resound. The inner music summons words. Arranges rhythms, harmonies. And found meanings.

That vibrate through awareness. Spoken.

3.

His fingertips, a feather tracing patterns on her belly. Radiating heat that travels. Her entirety responds. Awakening.

And she trembles as time dissolves.

4.

Jasmine, the scent caresses. Unlocks a distant memory, that moment of awe, as brief as it is eternal.

And once more she lives that sultry air, the entrance to the Shiva temple, the white blooms in little girl's hair. Superimposed on the now.

5.

The juicy sweetness on the tongue. Cherries, he feeds her cherries. One by one. And the flavor lingers long after he is gone away again.

Stretching the moment.

6.

Perceiving beauty in all forms. Communing with the world in reverence. Discovering that elusive resonance with deeper knowing.

An encounter that transcends.

CICADAS

1.

The pulsing song, the summer chorus, flamboyance of transitory joy. A boisterous celebration, long years in the making.

Vividly imagined in the dark. Imbibing the wisdom of the roots. Constructing mazes, labyrinths of hope, beneath the moist earth.

And then emerging, into the light, transforming. Shells cast off, acquiring new wings. Exploring with that five-eyed vision, ecstatic.

2.

Once mortals enchanted by the Muses, they sang ignoring sleep and hunger. Rejoicing when the metamorphosis occurred. Destined to sing their rhapsodies, however brief their time, with no distraction. Eternally enamored.

3.

Renowned for exuberant creation, sacred to both Dionysus and Apollo. Transcending boundaries of the self. And honoring precision of time's cycles.

Masters of pandemonium and order, their art supreme and simple, in praise of life.

HIS WORDS

1.

His words beckon from a distance, of space and time. A shared fantasy forged by longing. In the heat of summer. In the fires of faith.

2.

They embrace her, his words. And the senses sharpen. Awakening to possibility. Falling blissful into the unknown. The mystery of soulful desire.

3.

And the new light alters her seeing. Shades of green, swaying. Gentle as the breeze. As the clouds slowly transform, glowing. And miracles await.

SHAPESHIFTERS

1.

A cloud leisurely extends into possibility. Exploring the periphery. An image forms, almost. And just as gradually becomes another. Dissipates once more. Shifting in slow motion across the pale blue sky.

And thoughts too are evolving, pushing the boundaries of words. Leisurely, one shape begets another. Morphing, expanding meanings. Searching for resonance.

2.

When the sea-god Proteus approaches, time stands still. The only motion is the waves. Flowing only in perception. Shape shifting. Knowing all. Eluding questions. Of time past and future. Only the now is to be revealed.

3.

And then there is light. Transforming everything it touches. Recalling each object to itself. Releasing hidden knowing. From the oblivion of darkness. Returning.

Altered, in the clarity of encounter.

AN ENCOUNTER

1.

It is a form of preparation, this waiting. This silence. Creating space, for words to enter. A pause, charged with potential. A sacred time.

Of listening with all the senses. Welcoming.

2.

When they arrive, the words, they carry knowing. Messengers from the inner realms. Infused with otherness. The sense of beauty, sense of truth, revealing.

An encounter with the self.

3.

And as they are read, their meanings grow. Evolving through that encounter with another mind. Expanding the creative cycle.

Altering perception.

Notes on Previous Publication

Playing Times in Tongues, Part 1, was published by Verum Literary Press in August 2022.

Shifting Sands was published in Nine Cloud Journal in December 2022.

www.ingramcontent.com/pod-product-compliance
Lightning Source LLC
Chambersburg PA
CBHW071217120626
46546CB00006B/2605